Unlikely Glimpses of

Grace

J. Patrick Vaughn

ISBN-13: 978-0692341407
ISBN-10: 0692341404
LCCN: 2014958001

Cover and Interior designed by Ellie Searl, Publishista®

Chai Café Productions
Landenberg, PA

CONTENTS

Introduction *9*

Way, Truth and Life *11*

A Word about Heaven *13*

About That Serpent *14*

What Was Jesus Thinking? *15*

Spiritual but Not Religious *16*

Praying by Ourselves? *17*

Christianity under Attack? *18*

They Took Away Her Keys *19*

But What about Martha? *20*

A Mustard Seed *21*

In the Beginning *22*

Does God Speak to Us Today? *23*

Bartimaeus *24*

Building the Kingdom *25*

Evolution *26*

Glorify *27*

Reading Scripture *28*

Some of Jesus' Supporters *29*

The Power of Names *30*

Who Is the Central Character? *31*

The Virgin Mary *32*

VBS and the Trinity *33*

What Is the Secret of the Universe? *34*

Where Do You Encounter God? *35*

Who Are You? *36*

A Loving Parent? *37*

Does Sex Get Your Attention? *38*

Have You Ever Wondered? *40*

CONTENTS

Can You Be Bad at Praying? 41

Falling Asleep 42

Family Values 44

Getting Angry at Jesus 45

God's First Question 46

How Long Does God Look? 47

Shameless Love 48

The Chief Tax Collector 49

The Man and the Woman in the Garden 50

Jesus Praying on the Cross 51

Crucified, Dead and Buried 52

When We Don't Have Words 53

An Unlikely Bonus—Does God Ever Give Us More Than
     We Can Handle? 54

YouTube Links to "The Unlikely Minute" 57

For Mama and Daddy

Introduction

WHEN I ENTERED SEMINARY, I realized that I would be required to study the Bible and even learn a little Hebrew and Greek. But I really wasn't very interested in scripture. I looked forward to grappling with religious and philosophical themes and ideas.

As a matter of fact, when I was trying to decide where to attend graduate school, I had the opportunity to talk with a highly respected theologian. Given his acumen, I thought he would readily agree with me when I said, "Don't you think people just take the Bible too seriously?"

His response shocked me.

He took a puff on his pipe, smiled warmly, and replied, "No, not at all. I don't think most people take the Bible seriously enough."

After serving for more than twenty-five years as a pastor in Presbyterian churches, I continue to marvel at the wisdom of his words.

Far more than I ever imagined, scripture continually engages and startles me. It challenges me when I am a bit too comfortable or confident, and it offers hope and joy when I least expect it.

Instead of imparting information, scripture evokes transformation.

Instead of answering our questions, it questions our answers.

Instead of telling us what to believe (think), it points us to the One who risks rejection to believe (trust) in us.

The more I grapple with, resist, and digest the pages of scripture the more my eyes are opened to the unlikely grace of an unlikely God.

Just as it rained forty days and forty nights, as the children of Israel roamed for forty years, as Jesus struggled with temptation for forty days in the wilderness, and as Christians journey forty days through Lent to Easter, here you will encounter forty reflections on our unlikely God.

I hope you will be blessed in unexpected and unlikely ways.

Grace and peace,
Patrick

Way, Truth and Life

IN THE 14TH CHAPTER OF the Gospel of John, Jesus offers comfort to his disciples. He tells them, "Do not let your hearts be troubled. Believe in God. Believe also in me."

In that same passage he says, "I am the way and the truth and the life." He says these words as an expression of comfort and reassurance, but we often interpret them as words of exclusion.

"If you don't believe that Jesus is the way and the truth and the life, you are cast out! You are excluded! You are outside the love and acceptance of God!"

This. Is not. At all. What Jesus is teaching us!

When he says that he is the way and the truth and the life, he is saying that if we want to see who God is, if we want to peer into the inner character of God, if we want to catch a glimpse of God in the world, then we should look at his life and his ministry.

When we begin to look carefully at Jesus and listen to him, we behold how radically inclusive God's love is for us; for Jesus is the one who knocks down all kinds of social taboos and barriers to embrace Jew and Gentile, slave and free, male and female.

"I am the way the truth and the life." It's not about exclusion. It's a radical promise about inclusion. Now, that might seem unlikely, but it's good news.

A Word about Heaven

THE THEOLOGIAN REINHOLD NIEBUHR ONCE said that we shouldn't spend much time speculating about the furniture of heaven or the temperature of hell. Nevertheless, I, and I suspect you, sometimes wonder about heaven. What will it be like? Whom will we see? What will we do?

Scripture doesn't provide us with many details, but it does offer us an intriguing image. It says that heaven will be like a city. It will be "the new Jerusalem." So, imagine New York City, just for a moment. It's a bustling place, an active place with all kinds of people from all walks of life who speak in many different languages with many different accents with all kinds of things to do all day and all night.

That's not sitting all alone on a cloud, is it?

A city gives us an image of heaven that is so intriguing and exiting that it actually sounds rather unlikely!

About That Serpent

A FEW YEARS AGO, AS my wife and I were walking on a deserted dirt road in the mountains of Pennsylvania, we came across a five-foot long timber rattler. We both froze, scared to death.

I don't like snakes. I'm afraid of snakes. So when we come to the story about the serpent in the Garden way back at the beginning of Genesis, I'm prejudiced. I go into that story with a hatred and fear of snakes. They're bad. They're evil.

But that's not how Genesis describes the serpent in the Garden.

Genesis simply says that it was more crafty than all the other wild animals. The serpent is a trickster. The serpent is a troublemaker. He entices the man and the woman to sin.

Anything can be a serpent in our life. It can be a hobby. It can be a job. It can be a friend. It can be a form of entertainment. It can be the computer. It can be the television. Anything can entice us to pull away from God or pull away from our brothers and sisters and fracture our relationships with them. It doesn't have to be evil. It can just be tricky or crafty in its power and allure. How unlikely does that sound?

What Was Jesus Thinking?

SOMETIMES, I JUST DON'T UNDERSTAND Jesus. What was he thinking? What was going through his mind when he called together his disciples? He called Peter and Andrew. They were brothers. And when Jesus called them, immediately they left their nets and their father (!), and they followed Jesus.

He called James and John – they were mama's boys. He called Matthew – he colluded with the corrupt Roman Empire to cheat his neighbors. He called Judas – he was a "Zealot." Today, we would call him a terrorist or a freedom fighter.

He called together this incredibly diverse bunch of people. They had radically different perspectives, different attitudes, different ways of engaging the world. And yet, he somehow assembled them to learn together, walk together, eat together, grow together, serve together.

What could we learn from that example today, a day that is marked by Fox News on the one hand and MSNBC on the other? Hmm. It might be unlikely, but it might be helpful.

Spiritual but Not Religious

HAVE YOU EVER HEARD ANYONE say, "I'm spiritual, but not religious"? I have. And, for the most part, I really understand it and can appreciate the sentiment.

I have often reflected, "I'm spiritual. I want to have a relationship with God, but messing around with people, relating to people. Oh, I'm not sure about that. People will let you down. People will hurt you. People will sometimes even betray you."

The challenge for those of us in the Christian tradition, however, is that the Holy Spirit connects us to one another. In Acts and John we read about God breathing his Spirit upon his people, and in both accounts the Spirit sends us out into the world to tell others about God's love.

In the Christian tradition, there is no such thing as being spiritual but not religious. When the Holy Spirit comes, the spirit sends us out to meet others, to touch the lives of others, to learn from others, to see how God is at work in their lives. And then, together, we bear witness to God and worship God and rejoice in the good news that God loves us. That's unlikely for spiritual people, perhaps, but it's good news.

Praying by Ourselves?

A FRIEND ONCE ASKED, "IS it more effective for us to pray together rather than by ourselves?"

The answer is yes, absolutely! It is much more effective and faithful and meaningful for us to pray with one another.

Remember, Jesus teaches us to pray: *Our* Father, who art in heaven. Note that little word, "our."

In the New Testament, Paul writes all these letters to all these churches, all these gatherings, these communities of people. And most of the time in those letters, when he uses the word *you,* he really means y'all. It's the plural you, not the singular you.

Yes, we are much more likely to hear God speaking to us, to experience the grace and the love and the mercy and compassion of God when we are in relationships with our brothers and sisters.

Prayer is, after all, much more about God reaching out to us and speaking to us and engaging us and loving us rather than us speaking to God or asking something of God.

That might sound unlikely, but it's good news.

Christianity under Attack?

SOMETIMES, WE MIGHT WONDER, "WHY is Christianity under attack on so many different fronts?" After all, in certain parts of the world, Christians are suffering dire and painful persecution.

But when I consider the history of the church, and when I consider the church in North America today, I am much more concerned about internal decay than external threat.

The theologian Jürgen Moltmann once said that the cross is the test of everything that deserves to be called Christian. The cross: The radical display of God in the world for *all* people. Whenever the church forgets that God loves all people, rich and poor, gay and straight, first world and third world, when we forget that, we have forgotten our calling and our mission.

But when we remember the cross and we proclaim to the world the incredible love of God for each and every one, when we start doing that, oh, then, **then** we can expect persecution. When we love as Christ loved, we can expect be treated as Christ was treated.

I don't know about you, but I hope this remains an unlikely turn of events.

They Took Away Her Keys

I WAS ORDAINED WHEN I was only 24 years old. During my first year in ministry, I was asked by a senior citizen group to speak with them. I'll never forget what one woman said. She was in her mid-80s at the time. She said, "Patrick, I want to tell you what growing old means to me. It means that I can't drive anymore. They took my keys away. I can't drive anymore." Sorrow dripped from every word. She missed and grieved the ability to drive.

She spoke an important truth that day. As we get older, we do lose things that we value in our lives: the keys to our car, the ability to maneuver or get around as easily as we once did. We sometimes lose our eyesight. We sometimes even lose our memories.

I'm glad she shared that with me. It helps me to remember that whenever I am speaking with someone who is older than I am, whatever "older" means at that time, that if they are grumpy, or if they are repeating the same story again and again, they are just like me. I might not be there yet, but I will some day. And when that time comes, I will need someone to listen to me and walk beside me, hold my hand, and love me even as Jesus loves us.

But What about Martha?

THROUGHOUT THE CENTURIES, THE CHURCH has celebrated Peter's profound affirmation of faith. "Who do you say that I am?" Jesus asks Peter. Peter says, "I believe that you are the Christ." Just a few moments later however, Peter argues with Jesus about the kind of Christ Jesus would be.

We often hear about Peter, but I wonder why we rarely hear about Martha's profound affirmation of faith. In the 11th chapter of John, Martha chokes back tears as she grieves the death of her brother, Lazarus. Even though she is swallowed up by darkness and despair, she turns to Jesus, and she says, "I believe that you are the Christ, the one who is coming into the world." She affirms that Jesus is indeed the resurrection and the life. It is a stunning proclamation!

We hear about Peter, not so much about Martha. Why do we not hear about Martha? Is it because she's a woman? Is it because her profession of faith seems so unlikely?

A Mustard Seed

THROUGHOUT THE GOSPELS, JESUS USES a variety of images and stories to describe who God is and what God is about in the world. One of the most unusual of these images is that of the mustard seed. He says that the Kingdom of God is like a mustard seed.

Mustard? Mustard was considered to be a weed in the ancient world. It is much akin to what a dandelion or kudzu is to you and me today. It's a weed. It gets into areas where it does not belong, where it is not wanted. It stretches. It invades.

And that's the way God is today. God is ever-intervening, stretching, invading our world, and touching those places in our lives that we would rather keep God out of. Places like economics, social stratification, sexuality, international relations, politics. Oh, it's an unlikely image, this mustard. It's unsettling, and it might be good news too.

In the Beginning

The Bible opens with these words: "In the beginning, God created the heavens and the earth." You might have missed it, but this is a staggering affirmation of hope!

Written in the style of poetry, it is addressed to a time of great pain, suffering, and dislocation. An invading army had crushed Judah, and its leading citizens had been transported to Babylon.

Their world had been shattered, and they wondered, "Where is God? Has our God been defeated? Have we been abandoned by God?"

Over there on the shores of the Tigris and Euphrates Rivers, as they grieved, as they sank into despair, they developed this poetry, "In the beginning," "In the beginning." And they remembered that, indeed, God was the God not only of their tribe, not only of their nation, but the God of all the universe. Yes, even in their time of pain and suffering, even in their exile, God was with them. "In the beginning." A great message of hope, even if it does seem unlikely.

Does God Speak to Us Today?

CAN WE STILL HEAR GOD speaking to us today? Yes, we can. The challenge is to tune our ears to the sound of God's voice.

We hear God's voice when he tells Moses to go down to Egypt and liberate his people from slavery. We hear God's voice when his prophets chastise the people for ignoring the needs of the orphan, the widow, the foreigner, the outsider. We hear the sound of God's voice when Jesus cries in that stable. We hear the sound of God's voice when Jesus reaches out to the leper, the blind, the lame. We hear the sound of God's voice when Jesus says, "Let the little children come unto me."

Once our ears are tuned to the sound of God's voice, we will hear God speaking to us in a newscast, on a busy city street, out in the forest, in a conversation with a friend. We will hear God in the most unlikely of places.

Bartimaeus

IN THE GOSPEL OF MARK, Jesus heals person after person after person, but in only one situation do we discover the name of the person. Why?

His name is Bartimaeus, and Jesus gives him new sight. Bartimaeus means "son of Timaeus," and Timaeus is the name of an ancient Greek play.

Mark tells us that Bartimaeus casts off his cloak when he is healed. In the ancient world, the cloak was symbolic of a Greek philosopher, and in their worldview only men over the age of fifty could discern or understand truth.

Now, that cloak and its worldview have been discarded. With this miracle, Jesus is saying that no one is left out. All are welcome and all people can see and enjoy the truth of God. Does that seem unlikely to you?

Building the Kingdom

HAVE YOU EVER BEEN CHALLENGED to help build the Kingdom of God here on earth? Have you ever heard someone pray, "God, use these gifts that we might build your kingdom here"?

It sounds good. The problem, however, is that neither of these statements is biblical. I have made prayers like that. I have made statements like that. And then one day a wise teacher pointed out that this is not at all faithful to what Scripture teaches us.

Scripture says that we *receive* the Kingdom. Scripture says that we *enter* the Kingdom. The Kingdom of God, the rule of God, the realm of God in our midst is a gift. It's a presence. It's not something that we build up. It's a relationship into which we enter.

Have you thought about that lately? The Kingdom of God, the presence of God is God's gift to you. It sounds unlikely, doesn't it?

26

Evolution

D O YOU EVER GET TIRED of the creationist/evolutionist controversy? I do. I find it very, very wearisome. They're talking about two different issues all together.

Science asks, "How?" The Bible asks, "Who?"

The structure of the opening verses of Genesis is beautiful.

On day one, God creates light. On day four, God creates the sun and the moon. Days one and four parallel one another.

On day two, God separates the sky from the water. On day five, God creates the fish and the birds. Days two and five parallel each other.

On day three, God creates the land. And on day six, God creates wild animals. Days three and six parallel each other.

This is a stirring piece of poetry that praises God as the creator of all things. It's not answering the question of how. It's not addressing the Big Bang. It's affirming that ours is the God who created all that is. Does that seem unlikely to you? Maybe so, but it's good news.

Glorify

WHOM IN YOUR LIFE DO you glorify: your spouse, your children? Do you glorify your job? Do you praise or honor athletes or celebrities in the world today?

What does "glorify" really mean? To glorify is to show the essence of. To glorify is to reveal the character of. When we glorify God, we act or speak in such a way to show who God really is.

In the Gospel of John, Jesus says that he will glorify God through his suffering and death.

Consider that for a moment. It's in Jesus' suffering and death that he reveals the inner character of God, a God who is willing to suffer, and die, and be abused and tortured in order to be with us, to love us, to claim us.

Jesus glorifies God on the cross. That's an unlikely God.

Reading Scripture

"Twas the night before Christmas when all through the house…" I love that story. When I was growing up, we read it every Christmas Eve. We don't read that story, the same way we might read a Visa bill. And we don't read a Visa bill the same way we might read a note from our spouse saying, "I love you." We read different forms of communication in different ways.

Similarly, we read the Bible in different ways depending on which section we're in. The Bible is filled with stories, with parables. The Bible also has poetry and apocalyptic literature – which is a very strange kind of literature with all kinds of strange symbols.

We can't read the Bible from beginning to end in the same way. There are different genres of literature that evoke different responses in us, and it expects of us a different way of reading. We don't read poetry the same way we would read prose. Sound unlikely to you? Maybe, but it's good news.

Some of Jesus' Supporters

IN THE OPENING VERSES OF the eighth chapter of his Gospel, Luke mentions some of Jesus' supporters. They gave of their own resources to help provide for him.

Do you know who they were?

They were women.

Women supported Jesus. Women learned from Jesus. Women sat at the feet of Jesus and discovered the joy of faith. Jesus invited women into his presence in a time when they were not allowed to learn from a rabbi or speak to a man in public. It was strictly forbidden!

What does this tell us about Jesus, this unlikely messiah, this unlikely image of God?

The Power of Names

HAVE YOU GIVEN ANY THOUGHT lately to the meaning or the power of names? My middle name, for example, is Patrick, and Patrick means "noble." My first name is John. John means "God is gracious." The name Moses means "taken from the water."

What does God's name mean? In the Hebrew Scriptures, LORD, L-O-R-D, is often spelled with all capital letters. And when we see it spelled with all capital letters, this is a translation of a Hebrew name for God, Yahweh. Yahweh means, "I will be who I will be." This is the name that God revealed to Moses.

I will be who I will be. God's name, in other words, is a verb, and it'a not just any verb. It's a verb of causation.

God is the one who is actively engaged in, interfering with, and intervening in the affairs of the world. Ours is a living, active God. God's name is a verb. That's rather unlikely.

Who Is the Central Character?

WITH RUSSELL CROWE IN THE lead role, the movie *Noah* received all kinds of attention when it was released in 2014. It's filled with action and adventure and intrigue. There is the ark. There are the animals. There are the special effects. But in the midst of all this, who is really the central character?

According to the story we read in Genesis, God is the central character. When God looks upon creation and sees the evil and the wickedness of humanity, God is sorry that he made us. And then Genesis says something very, very interesting. It says that God is grieved. Grieved. That's the same word in ancient Hebrew that's used to describe women who are in the pain of labor.

When God beholds the way we treat one another with such disregard, when we harm one another, when we injure one another with our words or our actions or our tanks and guns, God is filled with deep, deep interior pain. That's an unlikely response from an unlikely God, a God who loves us with such passion that God feels pain when we hurt one another.

The Virgin Mary

"BORN OF THE VIRGIN MARY" is a phrase we find in the Apostles' Creed. Today, when we hear it, we tend to put the emphasis on the word *virgin*. But in the ancient world, the emphasis fell on the word *born*. Jesus was born just like you and me.

He did not materialize out of thin air. He did not fall out of heaven. He didn't pop out of the head of Zeus. No. Jesus was born.

He was fully human. He got tired. He got hungry. He got thirsty. He got frustrated. He slept at night. And, at the end of his life, he suffered and he died.

He died just as you and I will someday die. Jesus was fully human. He was born. Now, that's unlikely for a messiah, but it's good news because God comes to us as one of us.

VBS and the Trinity

IT WAS THE FIRST DAY OF vacation bible school, and I was walking around the church visiting each class. I entered one room, and the teacher said, "Patrick, come in. Come in." There was a bunch of nine and ten-year-olds sitting on the floor. The teacher said, "Patrick, would you please explain the doctrine of the Trinity to the children?"

What? Did I hear that correctly?

I said, "Sure."

I asked all the children to stand up in the center of the room. They held hands. And then I said, "All right. Hold hands. Dance to the right. Now dance to the left." We danced for several minutes.

I then added, "That's what God is like."

That really does help us to understand what the doctrine of the Trinity is all about. We can get confused in all kinds of theories, but at its heart the Trinity means that God's very nature is communal or social. God is ever reaching out to hold hands with more and more people and to dance through all eternity.

What Is the Secret of the Universe?

I HAVE A SIMPLE QUESTION for you. What is the secret of the universe? Have you given that any thought lately? For centuries, some people have looked at the entrails of animals or gazed into the heavens and studied the stars to try to figure out the meaning of life.

In the Gospel of John, however, we read in the first verse, "In the beginning was the Word." *Word* is not a very good translation of that term. The term is *logos*. And it's better translated as "ratio" or "proportion" or, better yet, "organizing principle."

In the beginning was the Organizing Principle, and that organizing principle became flesh and lived among us, and his name was Jesus.

What is the secret of the universe? What is the organizing principle of the universe? Well, we look to the life of Jesus, and we see in him someone who scandalized the good, religious folks of his day to love the unlovable, to touch the untouchable, and to accept the unacceptable.

That is the secret of the universe.

Where Do You Encounter God?

W HERE DO YOU ENCOUNTER GOD: in a sanctuary, a cathedral, a synagogue, by the shore when the waves are splashing? Maybe in a quiet forest, perhaps in a special room where you go to pray? Where do you encounter God?

When God approached Moses and told him to go down to Egypt and liberate his people from slavery, God did not wait until he was in a moment of prayer. He didn't go to Moses when he was in a religious tent. Instead, God went to Moses when Moses was going about his regular work.

He was in the family business. He was tending the sheep. He was a shepherd. And in that setting, God approached him, addressed him, engaged him, and sent him on a mission.

So if you are an accountant, a mortician, a doctor, a teacher, a student studying in a library, maybe you are retired; whenever you are going about your regular day's work that is where God might just come and encounter you. I know that might sound unlikely, but there is something joyful and uplifting about it too.

Who Are You?

WHO ARE YOU? IT'S A question I often ask when I meet someone for the first time. It's a strange question, I understand, but it's also rather disarming and usually puts the other person at ease.

A more difficult question would be, "Whose are you?" To whom do you belong? Do you belong to your family? Do you belong to your neighborhood? Do you belong to your class? Do you belong to your race? Do you belong to your nation? To whom do you belong? Whose are you?

In the Christian faith, we believe that, in life and death, we belong to God. God has claimed us. God loves us. And God will never let us go.

"Who are you?" That's a fun question to ask. "Whose are you?" can be difficult, but it brings with it this remarkable and unlikely good news. We belong to God.

A Loving Parent?

A FRIEND ASKED ME NOT too long ago if the church in other times in its history also understood God to be a loving parent. And the answer is, when the church has been at its best, when the church has been the most faithful, in those moments we have remembered and celebrated the good news that God is a loving parent.

Keep in mind, however, that love does not define God. God defines love. That is to say, we get our understanding of love not from our relationships, not from movies, not from television shows, not even from Hallmark cards. No, we get our understanding of love by reflecting on God's relationship with us. This God who goes down to Egypt to liberate his people from slavery. This God who goes into the exile of Babylon to embrace his people in their darkness and despair. This God who, in Jesus, touches lepers, and welcomes women, and forgives sins, and creates community.

What we see in God's relationship with us is a profound respect for our dignity. When we remember and act in such a way as to affirm and celebrate the dignity of others, even when they are different from us, then the church is at its best. And then we are being faithful to the God who loves us as a loving parent.

Does Sex Get Your Attention?

H AVE YOU EVER NOTICED HOW sex has a way of grabbing our attention? Of course you have. Sex is powerful, and that power was not lost upon the biblical writers.

Have you read the Book of Leviticus lately? Shake your heads back and forth. No one really reads the book of Leviticus, not very often anyway.

But if you do, you'll come to the 18th chapter, and there's a lot in the 18th chapter about sexuality. Don't uncover the nakedness of that person. Don't uncover the nakedness of this person. It'll get your attention.

And, then, the 20th chapter will also get your attention because it has all the penalties and the punishments for breaking the laws in the 18th chapter.

Eighteen and twenty, eighteen and twenty, they're all about sexual relationships. They get your attention. But if you keep reading the 18th and the 20th, pretty soon you'll end up reading the 19th.

And in the 19th chapter, we discover what it really means to be a holy people and worship a holy God. It tells us to honor our mothers and fathers. It tells us to take care of the poor and the resident alien. It tells us to honor the Sabbath. And right there, right there in the middle of the

19th chapter, we read this fascinating verse. It says we are to love our neighbor as we love ourselves.

The biblical writers knew what they were doing!

They get our attention with the 18th and the 20th. Those point us to the 19th and, right there in the middle of the 19th chapter, we come close to the heart of the Gospel: Love your neighbor as you love yourself.

That seems unlikely, but it's good news.

Have You Ever Wondered?

HAVE YOU EVER WONDERED, "WHY does God allow innocent people to die of starvation and other disasters, especially children?" There is no good or satisfactory answer to that question. Anything we say will simply leave us frustrated and perhaps even filled with despair.

It is worth remembering, however, that Jesus himself asks a very similar question. As he is about to die, he cries out on the cross, "My God, my God, why have you abandoned me?"

There is no answer. God does not speak. The silence is unbearable.

What this tells us is that when we are asking those questions, Jesus is with us. When we are raising our hands in rage and frustration with God, Jesus is with us. When we are questioning and doubting God, Jesus is with us.

God's love for us is so great that when we cry out, "Why, oh God, why have you abandoned us?" then (and maybe especially then?) Jesus is with us.

Why is there suffering? We do not know.

God does not give us an **answer**. Instead, God gives us an abiding and faithful **presence**.

Now that's unlikely, and that's good news.

Can You Be Bad at Praying?

SHANNON WIERSBITZKY IS A WONDERFUL writer of children's books. She is also a friend, and she once asked me, "Can a person be bad at praying?"

It will be helpful if we slightly reframe the question.

Can a person be bad at trusting? Can a person be bad at loving? Can a person be bad at caring?

If prayer were simply a matter of eloquence or a demonstration of one's wisdom, then yes, we could be bad at praying.

But prayer is the give and take between us and God. Prayer is about our relationship with God. Prayer is about trusting and celebrating the good news that, in Jesus Christ, God has claimed us and will never let us go. And upon that foundation, we develop our prayer life. We develop the ability to listen to God and respond to God.

Can a person be bad at praying? I don't know about that. But can we all learn? Can we all grow in our ability to love and listen and trust? Oh, yes, that we can do.

Falling Asleep

W HY DID THEY KEEP FALLING asleep? On the night that Jesus was arrested, he gathered a few of his disciples and went away to pray.

He asked them to stay awake while he was praying, but what did they do? They fell asleep. Why did they fall asleep? Could they not see the distress in his eyes? Could they not see the fear on his face? Could they not see the anxiety rippling through his body?

He was worried. He didn't want to die. He wanted that cup of sacrifice to be passed from him if it was God's will. But they fell asleep.

They fell asleep on Jesus in his hour of great urgency and need!

Why?

Before we get too hard on them, however, we might also want to consider why we fall asleep on God today. Do we not see the anguish, the despair, the worry on Jesus' face-

- ♦ when he beholds the hungry in the world, and the homeless,
- ♦ when he beholds children who have suffered at the hands of their parents,

♦ when he sees parents who have suffered elder abuse at the hands of their children,

♦ when he sees villages that have been bombed?

It seems unlikely, but Jesus might be asking us to stay awake with him even now.

Family Values

ARE FAMILY VALUES IMPORTANT TO you? They're important to me. I love my family.

But if we look to the pages of Scripture for guidance regarding family values, we will be very perplexed and confused.

Consider some of the stories. Cain kills his brother, Abel. Noah curses his son for something we really don't understand. Jacob tries to rip off his brother Esau. The stories of Scripture are filled with families that have been torn apart by jealousy, envy, and strife.

We turn then to the New Testament, and we hear Jesus say things like, "I've come to bring enmity between a parent and a child, between a brother and a sister." When Jesus' mother and brothers visit him, he says, "Well, who are my mother and my brothers and my sisters? Oh, the ones who do the will of God, they are my mother and my brothers and my sisters."

Instead of **family** values, Scripture points us to **kingdom** values, the values of mercy, peace, justice, love, reconciliation. And then, based on those values, we can build some family values. That might seem unlikely.

Getting Angry at Jesus

I CAN'T REMEMBER THE LAST time I was angry at Jesus. Can you remember the last time you were angry at Jesus? I wish I could remember, but I can't.

Now, I know that this will strike some as inappropriate to be angry at Jesus, but it seems to me that the capacity to be angry at Jesus requires a deep, deep faith. It requires faith that he is real. It requires faith that he loves us. It requires faith that he will intervene in our lives. It requires faith that he will make a difference in the way we live from day to day.

So then when we are disappointed, when that cancer is not healed, when that loved one has died, when we lose the job, when the wars around the world carry on, why don't we ever get angry at Jesus?

Sometimes I wonder how deep my faith really goes. Do you ever get angry at Jesus?

God's First Question

D O YOU RECALL THE FIRST question that God ever asks in Scripture? In Genesis 3 God asks, "Where are you?"

The man and the woman have eaten the forbidden fruit. They are ashamed. They feel lost. They have clothed themselves with fig leaves, and try to hide from God when they hear him heading their way.

Instead of shouting and screaming, God asks, "Where are you?" This is like a parent searching for a lost child. Where are you? Where are you? That's the question that God asks us even today.

Where are you? Oh, you are lost in an addiction.

Where are you? Oh, you're lost in a relationship with a spouse that is falling apart.

Where are you? Oh, the chemotherapy is difficult.

Where are you? Oh, you've been laid off.

Where are you? Oh, you've been the victim of violence.

Where are you? That's the question that God asks time and time again.

Where are you? It's an unlikely question.

How Long Does God Look?

IN THE 15TH CHAPTER OF Luke's Gospel, Jesus tells us several parables about being lost: a woman loses a coin; a shepherd loses a sheep. Do you remember how long they look for the lost? They look and look and look. How long? Until. Until they are found.

I love that word *until.* That's how long God looks for us. So when you are feeling as if you have lost your way; if you are feeling discombobulated in the world; if you are feeling dislocated; if you are feeling sort of disconnected from people, from life, from those around you; when you are feeling lost, remember that God is looking and looking and looking for you.

And God will look how long? Until.

Shameless Love

ARE YOU EVER SHAMELESS IN your love for God?
Jesus once told a story about a man who went to his
neighbor's house and knocked on the door, and knocked on
the door, and knocked on the door, until the neighbor gave
him some bread that he wanted to use to feed a guest who
had arrived unexpectedly.

Jesus says that because of the man's persistence, he was
granted his request. The word *persistence* is a weak
translation. It really means *shamelessness.*

The man was able to get the bread because he was
shameless in knocking on the door. He was shameless in
stirring up a commotion in that little village. He was
shameless in irritating his friends or causing a ruckus.

Are you ever shameless in your love for God? Are you
willing to knock on the doors of town hall, or your
neighbor, or corporate America to see to it that the hungry
are fed, or the naked are given clothing, or that the thirsty
are given drink, or that the imprisoned are visited? Are you
shameless in your love for God?

God is shameless in his love for us. Now, that might
seem unlikely, but it is good news.

The Chief Tax Collector

WHEN JESUS WAS PASSING THROUGH the village of Jericho, he came upon a man by the name of Zacchaeus. Well, he really didn't come upon him. Zacchaeus was hiding up in a tree.

Ostensibly, he was there so that he could get a better view of Jesus. But remember who Zacchaeus was. He was the chief tax collector, and that meant that he was the most hated man in all of Jericho.

He crawled up in that tree so he could hide from the crowd.

He was close enough to Jesus to see him, but not touch him. He was close enough to hear Jesus, perhaps, but not interact with him, not be transformed by him.

But what did Jesus do? He saw him in his hiding place, his place of security and safety, and invited him down and transformed his life.

Do you have a hiding place? I bet you do. We all have our hiding places, those places where we go to feel safe and secure. The next time you're there, do not be surprised if you hear Jesus calling out to you, inviting you to come down, to be with him, to have dinner by his side. It's an unlikely invitation, but it's wonderful, good news.

The Man and the Woman in the Garden

DO THE PAGES AND THE stories of Scripture ever seem far, far removed from your day-to-day life? Sometimes they strike me as remote, bizarre, strange; but, more often than I ever expect, they speak to our existence today.

Take the story of the man and the woman in the Garden. They ate the forbidden fruit. God found them. And then how did they respond?

The man said, "That woman," he pointed to the woman, "that you gave to me," he pointed to God, "she caused me to sin."

The woman said, "No, no, no, no, no, no," and she pointed to the serpent. "The serpent caused me to sin."

Neither one of them took responsibility for their own actions. The blame game was created in the Garden of Eden. How difficult it is for us today to take responsibility for our own actions when we hurt someone, or let somebody down, or have broken a heart, or have fractured a relationship!

The Bible was written thousands of years ago, and yet it still speaks to us today.

How unlikely is that?

Jesus Praying on the Cross

MANY YEARS AGO I READ that when Jesus was on the cross and he cried out, "My God, my God, why have you forsaken me?" it was the only time in his ministry when he prayed and referred to God as *God* rather than as *father*. Throughout his life, he knew God as an intimate presence, as his papa, as his daddy. But in his time of suffering and death, he felt absolutely abandoned such that he could only refer to God with that impersonal word *God* rather than *papa*.

That helps us to understand that in those moments when we feel abandoned, when we feel as if no one else understands us, when we are going through pain and suffering, and we feel as if God has abandoned us too, that Jesus is there. He's been there. He understands, and he'll never let us go.

Crucified, Dead and Buried

IN THE APOSTLES' CREED, WE say we believe that Jesus was crucified, dead, buried, and he descended into hell. All four phrases or words mean the same thing. Jesus was completely, fully, and wholly dead.

At the heart of our faith, however, is that powerful affirmation that God raised him up from the grave. This is good news. We do not believe that Jesus lived beyond the cross because of something inherent in him. Nothing within him survived his crucifixion. No, he was dead, completely dead.

But, by the grace of God, by the power of God, by the Spirit of God, God breathed into him new life. This gives us hope that when we too breathe our last, and when we are truly and fully and wholly and completely dead, we too will live again. Not because something within us will survive, but because of the grace and love of God. God loves us too much to leave us in a tomb. God will raise us up to love us, and embrace us, and invite us into his fellowship through all eternity.

When We Don't Have Words

IN THOSE MOMENTS WHEN WE have lost someone – a brother, a sister, a parent, a child – we often don't have the words to articulate our grief. We are overwhelmed with sorrow. Tears stream down, and we simply can not find the language to share with others the depths of our hurt.

Scripture, in these moments, provides us with such a word. It's a little word, and it's *amen.* Amen is the biblical way of saying "okay." Amen means, "Let it be." Amen is an affirmation of a word that has been spoken, a song that has been sung, or a life that has been well-lived.

So when we are grieving, and when the tears are flowing, or when we are sitting with someone who is trapped in the vice of grief, we can simply say: Amen.

Amen, we loved him.

Amen, she loved us.

Amen, God is present.

Amen, God will never let us go.

And, as we say, "Amen," we might just hear God whispering, "Amen" to us.

An Unlikely Bonus—Does God Ever Give Us More Than We Can Handle?

GOD DOESN'T GIVE YOU MORE than you can handle. Have you ever heard that? I bet you have. We hear it. Sometimes we even say it in times of distress: an economic setback, a divorce, an illness. God doesn't give you more than you can handle.

And my response to that is: Really? Really? God doesn't give us more than we can handle?

Can we think for a moment about the 20 million Russians who died under Stalin's reign? Could we think about the tens of thousands of Syrians who have now perished in the Syrian Civil War? Or let's talk about my grandfather just for a moment. I never knew him. He took his own life when my mother was 15 years old. Did God give him more than he can handle? Did God give him that struggle to begin with?

Therein lies our challenge with that saying, that favorite saying of so many people. What does it say about God? How do we know who God is and what God is about in the world?

Some people, for example, would say that we know about God from looking at nature. We look out the window, and we can see some snow. Sometimes the snow is beautiful.

There's a village in Switzerland by the name of Hohfluh. I love that little village. It's high up in the Swiss Alps with a deep valley below it. On the other side is a majestic mountain range. A bluish-grey glacier covers it, and it is absolutely astounding. And so sometimes when I look at nature, when I look at that mountain range, when I enjoy a sunset, I go, "God is kind and loving and gracious."

But if we're going to look at nature, we also need to think about earthquakes and hurricanes, and cells that multiply and mutate and turn into cancer.

Sometimes we think that God is good and kind and gracious because we consider our own experiences. We have been loved. We see other people loving one another, taking care of other people. We might, for example, talk about the works of Monet. I love the French impressionists, and I particularly enjoy Monet.

But if we're going to talk about Monet, maybe we also need to talk about some of the killers in history, some of the evil dictators like Stalin, like Hitler. If we base our understanding of God on who we are and our experiences of being human, we come up with a dead end. We cannot look to nature to determine who God is. We cannot trust our own experiences of humanity.

As Christians, we believe that the best guide to understanding God is Jesus. Jesus provides us the most faithful picture of God. And what do we learn about God in looking at Jesus? Jesus fed the hungry. Jesus healed the sick, even Peter's mother-in-law (Did you notice in the video I mistakenly said "his" instead of "Peter's"?) Jesus reached out so that all kinds of people would belong: foreigners, pagans, the hated Samaritans, and even women. In that day and time, spending time with women, talking with them in public was a deeply held taboo.

By the way, who were the first people to whom Jesus revealed himself on that Easter morning? Hmm. Women! Jesus wanted everyone to belong.

What do we learn about God when we look at Jesus? We see Jesus casting out demons and evil spirits. And, in our time, we can understand that to mean that Jesus gets rid of any power or force that would dehumanize us or ostracize us or punish us or label us because Jesus loves us.

Now, would that God send cancer into our lives or an economic setback? Would that God do that? I don't think so.

God doesn't give you more than you can handle. Well, God, if we look at Jesus' life, doesn't bring those things into our lives that take away from our life or break us or kill us. No, not at all.

YouTube Links to "The Unlikely Minute"

To SIGN UP FOR PATRICK'S biweekly vlog, "The Unlikely Minute," please go to www.theunlikelypreacher.com.

VISIT THE FOLLOWING YOUTUBE LINKS to view Patrick's vlog (video-blog) for each reflection in this book.

Way, Truth and Life
  http://youtu.be/lSAQwdRx5Wk

A Word about Heaven
  http://youtu.be/sNHtAxwWZXQ

About That Serpent
  http://youtu.be/VypLxqKTMrw

What Was Jesus Thinking?
  http://youtu.be/yMmwM7gs1lY

Spiritual but Not Religious
  http://youtu.be/7wB2PD7Onnc

Praying by Ourselves?
  http://youtu.be/nGinMMYUqVw

Christianity under Attack?
  http://youtu.be/u6hIbtkpQnQ

They Took Away Her Keys
http://youtu.be/nqckgo7cois

But What about Martha?
http://youtu.be/iRtkqtY9wjM

A Mustard Seed
http://youtu.be/XXuHyMiespE

In the Beginning
http://youtu.be/WVFkU4v17Ws

Does God Speak to Us Today?
http://youtu.be/4ra51nrWNd8

Bartimaeus
http://youtu.be/djDmUTTBE9E

Building the Kingdom
http://youtu.be/z8rt8TENOWE

Evolution
http://youtu.be/wJXy8golhwQ

Glorify
http://youtu.be/984xcTGZM5I

Reading Scripture
http://youtu.be/n7M3an9q9rc

Some of Jesus' Supporters
http://youtu.be/2wDQtjD7nU0

The Power of Names
http://youtu.be/s6G4yon3yng

Who Is the Central Character?
http://youtu.be/Y5EbKgE4zqc

The Virgin Mary
https://www.youtube.com/watch?v=n3Pj
LR7TZyw

VBS and the Trinity
http://youtu.be/4q_PhAopwYs

What Is the Secret of the Universe?
http://youtu.be/prhfD1y8RhE

Where Do You Encounter God?
http://youtu.be/eMqpsC9-NKg

Who Are You?
http://youtu.be/of2Pf7VvWq8

A Loving Parent?
http://youtu.be/L3ingfQF2UE

Does Sex Get Your Attention?
 http://youtu.be/Pgx4fw8IQms

Have You Ever Wondered?
 http://youtu.be/F-I3oNCjOvE

Can You Bad at Praying?
 http://youtu.be/3IV2oVZg6Ds

Falling Asleep
 http://youtu.be/wnCj5afBH3o

Family Values
 http://youtu.be/HJUScV1MnFI

Getting Angry at Jesus
 http://youtu.be/d1KDJiYJKPU

God's First Question
 http://youtu.be/eAbYj7ws_iM

How Long Does God Look?
 http://youtu.be/PwpxDV-mIMo

Shameless Love
 http://youtu.be/1Aa4Isi_F4k

The Chief Tax Collector
 http://youtu.be/zwn7R8Lbo8s

The Man and the Woman in the Garden
   http://youtu.be/SSkw1W-SpIs

Jesus Praying on the Cross
   http://youtu.be/wGo5YApXFIU

Crucified, Dead and Buried
   http://youtu.be/sTZd5dwoPJ8

When We Don't Have Words
   http://youtu.be/qW-r4xh1fMU

An Unlikely Bonus—Does God Ever Give Us
   More Than We Can Handle?
   http://youtu.be/GW8j82j2PBA